Girls Play to Win

VOLLEYBALL

by Chrös McDougall

Content Consultant
Mike Hebert
Head Coach
University of Minnesota
Volleyball

NORWOOD HOUSE PRESS
CHICAGO, ILLINOIS

Norwood House Press
P.O. Box 316598
Chicago, Illinois 60631

For information regarding Norwood House Press, please visit our website at:
www.norwoodhousepress.com or call 866-565-2900.

Photo Credits: Jamie Schwaberow/NCAA Photos/AP Images, cover, 1; iStockphoto,
cover, 1; Shutterstock Images, cover, 1, 7, 11, 14, 17, 24, 25, 27; Robert F. Bukaty/AP
Images, 4; Pavel Losevsky/Fotolia, 12; Library of Congress, 18; AP Images, 21, 37, 57;
N. Masaki/AP Images, 28; Zheng Xun/AP Images, 31; Beth A. Keiser/AP Images, 34;
Bob Galbraith/AP Images, 38; Roxanne McMillen/Shutterstock Images, 42; Laurent
Rebours/AP Images, 47; Andy Wong/AP Images, 48; Koji Sasahara/AP Images, 51;
Andy Wong/AP Images, 52; Christopher Halloran/Shutterstock Images, 55; Chrös
McDougall, 64 (top); Mike Hebert, 64 (bottom)

Editor: Melissa Johnson
Designer: Christa Schneider
Project Management: Red Line Editorial

Library of Congress Cataloging-in-Publication Data

McDougall, Chros.
  Girls play to win volleyball / by Chros McDougall.
    p. cm. — (Girls play to win)
  Includes bibliographical references and index.
  Summary: "Covers the history, rules, fundamentals and significant
personalities of the sport of women's volleyball. Topics include:
techniques, strategies, competitive events, and equipment. Glossary,
Additional Resources and Index included"—Provided by publisher.
  ISBN-13: 978-1-59953-392-6 (library edition : alk. paper)
  ISBN-10: 1-59953-392-8 (library edition : alk. paper)
  1. Women volleyball players—Juvenile literature. I. Title.
  GV1015.4.W66M365 2010
  796.325082—dc22
                    2010009810

Manufactured in the United States of America in North Mankato, Minnesota.
183R—042011

Girls Play to Win

VOLLEYBALL

Table of Contents

▲ Lang Ping (fourth from left) with the U.S. women's indoor volleyball team

CHAPTER 1

PASS, SET, HIT!

Some call her the Michael Jordan of China. Just as Jordan symbolizes U.S. basketball, Lang Ping is the face of Chinese volleyball. Lang, who also goes by "Jenny," led the Chinese team to Olympic gold in 1984. She became a superstar overnight. She later explained what the win meant to her country: "At that time China wasn't an open door to the world. But since then the Chinese people believe that we can do well. And not just in sports."

Lang's example encouraged Chinese athletes in all sports to strive for international excellence. She became so famous that her image was put on a postage stamp and her wedding was broadcast on television. She moved to the United States in the 1990s so she could live more privately.

After she retired as a player, Lang went into coaching. She became the head coach of the U.S. women's indoor team. She was the only woman coaching a top-20 team at the time. She returned to China for the 2008 Summer Olympics in Beijing—leading the U.S. team against her native country. Her Chinese fans didn't seem to mind too much, however. She was greeted with cheers and photographers, and spectators chanted her old nickname, "Iron Hammer," as the U.S. team played its way to a silver medal. It was a triumphant homecoming for one of China's favorite daughters.

PLAYING THE GAME

Basic volleyball is easy to play. All you need are some friends, a ball, and a net. You can play it almost anywhere, too. Organized volleyball is played in a gym or on a beach. But many people play at a park or in their backyards.

Volleyball began in a gym about 100 years ago. The indoor version of the sport is still popular. Volleyball is played on a rectangle-shaped court. A net divides the court in two. Teams of six players stand on each side of

The Six Basic Volleyball Skills

Attack: An offensive shot to the other team's court that is often a **spike** or a **dink**.

Block: When a spike is stopped by the extended arms of one or more frontline defenders who jump at the net.

Dig: Stopping the ball from touching the floor or ground after an opponent's attack shot.

Pass: When a team receives the serve and directs the ball to the setter.

Serve: The first contact of a rally, it can be done underhand, overhand, or by jumping.

Set: Usually the second contact by a team, it is a soft hit that places the ball for an attacking shot.

the net. Each team tries to hit the ball over the net and onto the other team's side. The goal is to "ground" the ball, or have it land, in the opponent's court.

A **rally** begins with a **serve**. A player hits the ball from the back of her court. If the serve is successful, the ball shoots over the net. Now the other team tries to return it. Each team may contact the ball three times before sending it over the net. The players are not allowed to catch or

▲ *The player on the left is serving to start the rally.*

Volleyball Lingo

Ace: When the serve itself wins a point.

Assist: A pass or set to a teammate that results in a kill.

Double hit: A foul that occurs when a player hits the ball twice in a row, unless the first touch was a block.

Kill: A shot that wins a point by landing in the other team's court.

Rally: The time in a volleyball game beginning with the serve and ending when the ball goes out of play.

Set: A single volleyball game.

hold the ball. Also, no player may touch the ball two times in a row.

The rally ends when the ball goes out of play. A team scores a point by grounding the ball in the other team's court. A team also can score if the opposing team sends the ball out of bounds or into the net, or if it hits the ball illegally. The team that wins the rally also gets the next serve.

A single volleyball game is called a set. A team wins a set when it is first to score 25 points. The winning team must have at least two more points than the other team. If the score is tied or close, the teams continue playing beyond 25 points. One team must be ahead by at least two points to win.

Teams play several sets to decide the winner of the match. In indoor volleyball, a team must win three out of five sets. If the teams have won two sets each, the last set is played to 15 points, not 25. The winner still needs a two-point lead to win.

VOLLEYBALL MOVES

Players can serve in three different ways. Some hold the ball in one hand and swing the other arm to strike the ball underhand. Others toss the ball into the air and hit it above their body. Some **elite** players use a jump serve. They toss the ball into the air in front of them. Then they run forward and jump to strike the ball. The jump serve is the most difficult, but it is also the most powerful.

Once the ball is served, the rally is underway. Each rally is unique. However, most rallies follow the formula of **pass**, **set**, and **attack**.

A pass is often the first contact when a player receives the serve. This contact, which is made using the forearms, is a good defensive technique. The second teammate receives the pass with a set. The set is a soft, overhead contact by the player's spread hands. The set puts the ball into position for an attack. The attack is often a spike, which is a hard, driving blow toward the opponent's floor.

Not all plays follow the pass-set-attack pattern. Players often have to **block**. When one team spikes the ball,

Professional Indoor Volleyball

In the United States, most indoor volleyball players start competing in college. Indoor volleyball is a National Collegiate Athletic Association (NCAA) sport at many colleges and universities across the country. Skilled college players are sometimes invited to join the U.S. Olympic team.

The United States does not have a **professional** indoor volleyball league for players to join after college. Many star U.S. players join professional indoor leagues in other countries. They temporarily return to the United States if they are selected for the U.S. Olympic team, however.

front-row players on the other team try to block it. They block by holding their arms up and jumping at the net.

Another important move is the **dig**. If the spike gets past the blockers, a back-row player can save it with a dig. This can be done with any part of the body. Sometimes, it is similar to a pass. Other times, a player tries to get any body part under the ball and keep it airborne.

Young players who are unable to spike the ball use other shots to hit the ball over the net. A soft shot that goes above or around the other team's blockers is called a dink. Using a soft hit when the opponent is expecting a spike is called a dump.

▲ *Frontcourt players block the ball.*

The six players start lined up in the front and back rows.

INDOOR VOLLEYBALL POSITIONS

Frontcourt Players

Outside hitter: *Receives serves and attacks balls that are set to her on the left side.*

Right side hitter/Opposite: *Attacks balls on the right side and is rarely needed for passing duties.*

Middle blocker: *Attacks from the middle front and is the primary blocker on defense.*

Backcourt Players

Setter: *The playmaker, she creates attacking opportunities.*

Specialty Players

Frontcourt players who struggle with serving, passing, and defense are often replaced in the backcourt by these players.

Defensive specialist: *Receives serves and digs balls to the setter.*

Libero: *This defensive player wears a different colored shirt. She can be substituted into the backline at any time but cannot attack a ball.*

INDOOR POSITIONS AND ROTATION

Most indoor volleyball teams have six players, each with a special position. Each position requires a different set of skills. For example, some positions specialize in frontcourt play, such as blocking and spiking. Others are mostly in the back. Backcourt players receive serves and dig spikes. There are more members on the team than can play at the same time. This means the coach can substitute different players in different situations.

Indoor players have to be **versatile**, too. When a team wins the serve, all of the players rotate one position clockwise. Rotating makes sure that every player serves. Some players are allowed to move to their usual positions after the serve.

BEACH VOLLEYBALL

Volleyball was first played indoors on a hard court. It soon became a popular game on the beach, too. Today, both types of volleyball are played in the Olympics. The traditional sport and the beach version share the same basic skills. However, there are major differences between the two types of volleyball.

Indoor games are played on a court made of wood or another floor material. Beach games are played on sand. These surfaces change the style of game play. Indoor games are known for being fast. The athletes move quickly across the court and jump high to spike and block. Players

▲ This player is performing a jump serve.

Indoor versus Beach
(in women's international competition)

Number of Players
   Indoor: Six each
   Beach: Two each

Court
   Indoor: 59 feet (18 m) long, 29 feet (9 m) wide
   Beach: 52.5 feet (16 m) long, 26.25 feet (8 m) wide

Scoring
   Indoor: Best of five sets. First four games are played to 25 points; the fifth game is played to 15.
   Beach: Best of three sets. First two games are played to 21 points; the third game is played to 15.

on sand cannot move as quickly. They have to work harder to move and jump. Playing outdoors also means the players have to adapt to the elements. They can use the sun and wind to their advantage—or these elements can work to their disadvantage. Outdoor players also compete in swimsuits because of the heat and sand.

Another major difference between the two versions is the size of the teams. Each beach volleyball team has only two players. If one gets tired, she does not have a substitute to relieve her. Since beach volleyball teams have fewer players, their strategy is different. Indoor players sometimes specialize in one area of play, such as blocking

Professional Beach Volleyball

Beach volleyball was scheduled to become an NCAA sport in the 2010–11 season. College athletes prior to this played on indoor teams or played for fun only.

Unlike indoor volleyball, beach volleyball has several professional tours in the United States, as well as international events. These tournaments are held by volleyball associations such as the Association of Volleyball Professionals (AVP) and the Fédération Internationale de Volleyball (FIVB).

or defense. Beach volleyball players move around more and have to play all positions.

Another difference is the length of the games and the match. Beach volleyball games are often shorter than indoor games. Beach volleyball matches are played to the best of three games. The first two are played to 21 points, with a minimum two-point lead needed to win. The third game is played to 15 points, also with a minimum two-point lead to win. The court is smaller, too.

▲ U.S. beach volleyball player Nicole Branagh digs the ball during a competition in 2009.

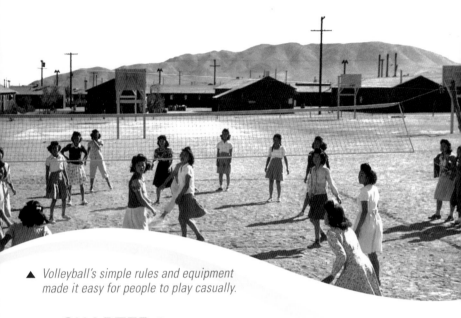

▲ *Volleyball's simple rules and equipment made it easy for people to play casually.*

CHAPTER 2

ORIGINS
OF THE GAME

The origins of volleyball are closely linked to the creation of basketball. James Naismith invented basketball in 1891. He was working at the Young Men's Christian Association (YMCA) Training School in Springfield, Massachusetts. It was a popular game, but the sport was too physical for some people. There were few indoor sports that people could play during the cold winters.

William G. Morgan wanted to change that. The young man had been a football player under Naismith at the YMCA Training School. By 1895, Morgan was director of physical education at the YMCA in Holyoke, Massachusetts. Morgan wanted to create a simple game that could be played year-round. The sport he invented was called mintonette. He refined the sport over the next several years into what we know as volleyball. Within only a few years and a few miles of each other, two of the most popular sports in the world were born.

Mintonette was a simple game. Teams stood on opposite sides of the net and hit the ball back and forth. There was no set number of players per team. Each team could hit the ball as often as needed. The goal was to ground the ball on the opponent's court. The basics were much the same as they are today.

Mintonette

When William G. Morgan created mintonette, it was a combination of many other sports. The net came from badminton, and the ball was similar to a basketball. Instead of sets, they played innings, similar to baseball—one team served until it made three outs. And players used their hands to hit the ball, just as in handball.

In 1896, Morgan demonstrated the sport to YMCA directors of physical education. They noticed that it involved volleying, or hitting the ball before it touched the ground. This helped change the sport's name to volley ball, which eventually became a single word, volleyball. After the meeting, the YMCA directors adopted common rules for volleyball. They began introducing the sport at YMCA and Young Women's Christian Association (YWCA) locations around the world.

Timeline of Major Indoor Rule Changes

1912—Each team has six players, and only three hits are allowed per team.

1912—Player rotation is introduced.

1922—Teams must win by two points.

1935—Touching the net for any reason becomes a foul.

1947—Only frontline players are allowed to block.

1976—Measurements switch to the metric system and matches are played to best of five games.

1999—Rally scoring is introduced, and games are played to 25 points.

▲ *Volleyball was first played at the Olympics in 1964. The Japanese women's team won the gold medal.*

THE SPORT GROWS

Missionaries associated with the YMCA and YWCA began teaching the game all around the world. The sport soon spread to Canada, Cuba, Japan, China, the Philippines, and other countries. It was introduced to Great Britain and other parts of Europe around 1914. U.S. soldiers fighting in World War I played while stationed overseas. The game continued to spread throughout Europe after the war ended in 1918.

There were some differences in volleyball around the world. In Japan, each team had nine players. In the United States, each team had six players. But the basic concept of the game was largely the same.

During its early years, volleyball was played mostly for fun. People began to take it more seriously as the sport

Indoor Volleyball Championships

In addition to the Olympics, there are three other major international volleyball competitions. The earliest was the World Championship, which began for women in 1952. The event is held every four years. Volleyball has been played in the Olympic Games, which are also held every four years, since 1964. A third major tournament, the World Cup, began in 1973. It, too, is held every four years. In 1993, the World Grand Prix began. It is an international tournament that takes place every year. Since the 1960s, Japan, Russia (the former Soviet Union), China, and Cuba have had some of the strongest women's volleyball teams.

became increasingly popular. Some of the first major tournaments in the United States were organized during the 1920s. The first national volleyball **federations** began forming during the 1920s and 1930s. These federations organize the sport in their countries. They make sure everybody plays by the same rules.

The game evolved during this time, as well. In 1920, players from the Philippines began using an early form of the spike. In 1938, the Czechs mastered blocking.

During the 1940s, U.S. servicemen stationed overseas during World War II helped spread the game even further. Volleyball took a big step toward becoming a major world sport after the war. In 1948, 14 nations came together to create the *Fédération Internationale de Volleyball* (FIVB), or International Federation of Volleyball. The FIVB organized and governed the sport around the world.

In 1949, the United States began offering a women's national championship tournament. In 1952, the first women's world championships took place. Volleyball **debuted** as a medal sport for men and women at the 1964 Olympics in Tokyo, Japan. It has been a popular Olympic sport ever since.

BEACH VOLLEYBALL

As volleyball grew more popular and competitive, a new version of the sport began to develop. Some people believe beach volleyball originated in Hawaii during the 1920s. However, most people accept that the first games were held in Santa Monica, California, around the same time. The sport spread to France in 1927. Soon, other Europeans were playing.

The first beach volleyball games often had teams of six players. By the 1930s, two-person teams began to appear on the beaches of Southern California. People still played on teams of all sizes, though. The first official two-person tournament took place in 1947. But the winner received no prize money. Early beach volleyball tournaments were often held by local parks or recreation associations. Winners were often happy to win a new outfit or a free dinner.

▲ *People around the world love to play beach volleyball, like these players in Australia.*

Beach volleyball grew in popularity during the 1970s. The first professional tour was created in 1976. More than 30,000 people attended. Events soon took place around the United States. The increased popularity drew **sponsors**, and players began receiving prize money. Beach volleyball, like surfing, had become an important part of California's beach culture. At this time, women played in exhibition games as a side event to the men's games.

To help the sport grow, the Association of Volleyball Professionals (AVP) organized a U.S. tour. This brought more money to the sport. Professional female players created their own organization in 1986: the Women's Professional Volleyball Association (WPVA). The WPVA's tour never became well established, and the WVPA folded in 1997. Today, most professional U.S. men and women players compete in the AVP tour.

Players compete in the 2007 FIVB World Tour.

BEACH VOLLEYBALL COMPETITIONS

*The FIVB holds a World Tour each year. It also holds the World Champi-
onships every other year. The top athletes in the world compete in these
events. The results in the World Championships and World Tour determine
which teams can compete in the Olympics. There are also cash prizes.*

*In the United States, the AVP holds two tours, as well. They are the AVP
Pro Beach Volleyball Tour and the AVP Hot Winter Nights Indoor Tour. Many
U.S. athletes compete in the AVP to earn money. AVP wins have no effect
on who participates in the Olympics.*

WORLDWIDE APPEAL

Beach volleyball spread to Brazil as early as the 1950s. Brazilians enjoy warm weather and many beaches in their country, so they embraced the sport. By the 1980s, it was popular in Australia, as well. Along with the United States and Brazil, Australia was an early power in the sport.

Beach volleyball tournaments became more popular across the United States and the world. Prize money and sponsorships increased during the 1980s and early 1990s. Some of the tournaments were broadcast on major television networks, including ESPN and NBC. The FIVB created its own world tour for women in 1992.

Finally, in 1996, beach volleyball truly became a mainstream sport. That year, it debuted at the Olympic Games in Atlanta, Georgia. The sport was a hit with spectators. Afterward, a reporter for *Sports Illustrated* wrote, "Indoor volleyball, which never again will be known as real volleyball, is going to have to find some flourishes of its own to keep pace with the upstart California game." In 2008, approximately 4.2 million people played beach volleyball in the United States.

▲ *This Huntington Beach, California, event is part of the AVP Pro Beach Volleyball Tour.*

▲ *The Japanese team beat the Soviet team at the 1964 Olympics.*

CHAPTER 3

STARS
ON THE COURT

The 1964 Olympics were held in Tokyo, Japan. It was the first time that indoor volleyball was an Olympic medal sport. Japan had the best women's volleyball team in the world that year. They had won more than 130 matches in a row coming into the Olympics. Now, they had a chance to win Olympic gold.

The Japanese women's team was unlike any other volleyball team in the world. Coach Hirofumi Daimatsu was very demanding of his players. The best 16 players lived, worked, and trained together. Six days each week, they would wake up at 7:00 a.m. They worked in a textile plant from 8:00 a.m. until 3:30 p.m. From 4:00 p.m. until 12:00 a.m., they practiced **intensely** with Daimatsu. He taught them to dive across the court and sacrifice their bodies to make a dig. They had little free time: only Sundays and one week off each year.

Japan's only strong challenger at the Olympics was expected to be the Soviet Union's team. The Soviet Union once included Russia and several other Eastern European countries. It broke apart in 1991. As many as 95 percent of television viewers in Japan tuned in for the gold-medal game. The home team did not disappoint, and Japan won in three sets. As a *New York Times* reporter described,

The Rolling Receive

Hirofumi Daimatsu, the coach of Japan's 1964 Olympic team, was tough on his players. He was also innovative. Daimatsu is credited with inventing the rolling receive move. This move involves a player diving to dig the ball, rolling over in a somersault, and returning to her feet. Done correctly, the move allows a player to reach faraway balls without hurting herself. She can recover quickly to be ready for the next play.

"These girls have made the familiar playground game a bruising competition in which it is common for a player to be sent spinning, heels over head, by a bulletlike shot."

A SOVIET FORCE

The Japanese team dominated from 1960 to 1965. That team was named best of the century by the FIVB in 2000. But the Soviet Union's team soon caught up. Inna Ryskal led the way as the Soviet team won the 1968 Olympics, 1970 World Championship, and 1972 Olympics. The team also won the first World Cup in 1973.

Ryskal was the ultimate power hitter on a squad known for power hitting. She began playing at age 12 and joined the Soviet junior national team by age 15. One year later, in 1961, she became a member of the national team. She played in the next four Olympics—1964, 1968,

Takako Shirai

Takako Shirai led a second generation of Japanese indoor volleyball teams to international success. Shirai joined Japan's national team for the 1972 Olympics in Munich, West Germany. Her powerful spikes and strong blocking helped Japan win a silver medal. She won gold medals at the 1976 Olympics, 1974 World Championship, and 1977 World Cup before retiring in 1978.

▲ Lang Ping led China to success in the 1980s. Above, Lang returns to China in 2009 to accept a coaching position.

1972, and 1976. The Soviet women won two gold medals and two silver medals during that time. The two silver medals were the result of losses to Japan.

GO, CHINA!

No team could match China in the early 1980s. Between 1981 and 1986, China won two World Cups (1981 and 1985), two World Championships (1982 and 1986), and one Olympic Games (1984).

Lang Ping was China's captain and star player. Lang was a powerful outside hitter. She joined China's national team at age 18 in 1978 and played until 1985. While Lang was on the team, China won first place at the 1981 and 1985 World Cups, the 1982 World Championship, and the 1984 Olympics. China was the defending Olympic, World, and World Cup champion. Lang dominated in the gold-medal match at the 1984 Olympics. China defeated the United States in all three sets. Lang retired after winning the World Cup and the Most Valuable Player award in 1985. But she briefly returned in 1990 to help China's team win the World Championship.

Lang's powerful spikes captivated fans in her country. She became a national superstar after the team won a gold medal at the 1984 Olympics. The game was broadcast throughout China. Afterward, fireworks filled the sky in Beijing, the nation's capital. One diplomat at the U.S. embassy said he had never seen such a public display of emotion in the country. Many Chinese became volleyball fans because of Lang and her 1984 team.

1924 Olympics

Volleyball officially became an Olympic sport in 1964. But it was first played at the 1924 Olympics in Paris, France, where it was a demonstration event. Volleyball was showcased as part of a U.S. sports demonstration—it was not a part of the official program and no medals were awarded.

In the 1990s, Lang became the first woman to coach the Chinese team. During her time as coach, China won a bronze medal at the 1995 World Cup, a silver medal at the 1996 Olympics, and a silver medal at the 1998 World Championship. Then she coached the U.S. team to a silver medal at the 2008 Olympics in Beijing. After the 2008 Olympics, Lang accepted a coaching position in China.

SENSATIONAL CUBA

Cuba surprised Japan and the Soviet Union by winning the 1978 World Championship. Some people believe Cuba would have won more medals in the 1980s if the nation had not **boycotted** the 1984 and 1988 Olympics. Cuba won its first World Cup in 1989 and was almost unstoppable from 1991 until 2000. The team won three more World Cups (1991, 1995, and 1999), two World Championships (1994 and 1998), and three Olympic gold medals (1992, 1996, and 2000). Mireya Luis and Regla Torres played on all three of Cuba's winning Olympic teams.

Luis began playing volleyball when she was ten and joined the national team at age 15. Luis was an exciting player to watch. She was 5 feet 10 inches (1.78 m) tall, which is fairly short for a volleyball player. But Luis was an amazing jumper. With a 36-inch (0.91 m) vertical leap and a powerful spike, Luis was one of the best players of all time. She was very popular during the 1990s and inspired many people to start playing volleyball.

▲ Cuban player Regla Torres spikes the ball while playing against the Brazilian team during a semifinal match at the 2000 Olympics.

"The Golden Lefty"

Cecilia Tait played Olympic volleyball three times for Peru. "The Golden Lefty," as she was known, was most memorable in her final Olympic Games in 1988, in Seoul, South Korea. Tait captivated Peruvians as her strong spikes led Peru past the favored teams from Japan, the United States, and China. Peru lost to the Soviet Union in the gold-medal game.

Tait learned to play volleyball in the streets. By the end of her career, many considered her to be the best player in the world. Tait became a politician after retiring in 1998, serving in the Peruvian Congress. She continues to inspire young girls to take up volleyball.

Torres was a more versatile player. She began playing volleyball when she was eight years old. When she was 14, at the 1992 Olympics, Torres became the youngest volleyball player to win a gold medal. A middle blocker and hitter, Torres was known for strong serving and blocking. The FIVB named Torres the best female volleyball player of the century in 2000.

THE U.S. TEAM

The U.S. team did not have much success in early Olympics. The U.S. team finished fifth out of six teams when the sport made its Olympic debut in 1964. Compared to Japan and other teams, the U.S. team did not seem prepared. The team also was weak on defense.

Coaches borrowed elements from Japan's intense training and tried to adapt them for U.S. players. The U.S. women's team began living together and training year-round in 1978. It was the first U.S. Olympic team to do so.

The 1984 Olympics were in Los Angeles, California. Led by Flo Hyman, the U.S. women won a silver medal. The U.S. team defeated China 3–1 earlier in the tournament. But China won 3–0 in the gold-medal game.

Hyman was 6 feet 5 inches (1.96 m) tall. She was considered the best player in the world at the time. "The audience would hold its breath when she rose for a spike," described one sportswriter. Hyman died two years after the Olympics, at age 31, from a rare genetic disorder.

The U.S. women's team went on to win a bronze medal at the 1992 Olympics in Barcelona, Spain, and a silver medal at the 2008 Olympics in Beijing, China. The team also won a silver medal at the 2002 World Championship.

▲ Flo Hyman helped the U.S. team win a silver medal at the 1984 Olympics. Above, posing in San Juan, Puerto Rico, in 1979.

▲ Brazilian fans cheer their beach
volleyball team at the 1996 Olympics.

CHAPTER 4

STARS
ON THE SAND

The beach volleyball community had good reason to be excited in 1996. The sport had grown steadily for more than a decade. People in dozens of countries around the world were playing organized beach volleyball. Major tours emerged in the United States and other nations.

WELCOME TO ATLANTA

Beach volleyball became an official Olympic sport in 1996. The Olympics were held that year in Atlanta, Georgia. A total of 600 athletes from 42 countries competed for spots in the volleyball competition. The sport's first Olympic appearance featured 18 women's teams. Some countries sent more than one team.

There were no beaches in Atlanta, however. So, organizers built a beach volleyball stadium approximately 20 miles (32 km) away from the Olympic Stadium. With a sand court and barefoot players wearing swimsuits, sunglasses, and sunscreen, the stadium felt like a real beach.

The entire beach volleyball competition lasted six days. The 10,000-seat stadium was sold out for all of the matches. Fans waved flags and cheered on their favorite players. During breaks, onlookers danced and sang along to the rock music blaring over the loudspeakers. "If the enthusiasm of today's fans, both old and new, was any

The Sport Grows Up

"I was out there in the old days playing for T-shirts and dinners. To be out there now, not only making a living but being an Olympian, you can't ask for anything more."

Linda Hanley, Team USA, 1996

gauge, the rapidly growing sport is finally being taken seriously some 66 years after its invention in the sands of Santa Monica," a *New York Times* reporter wrote.

BRAZIL STARS

The top beach players came from Brazil, Australia, and the United States, specifically California. In the gold-medal game, Brazilians Sandra Pires and Jackie Silva defeated another Brazilian team. A team from Australia won the bronze medal. U.S. teams came in fourth and tied for fifth place. Pires, Silva, and bronze medalists Adriana Samuel and Monica Rodrigues became heroes in Brazil. They were the first Brazilian women to medal at an Olympics.

Silva began playing on the Brazilian beaches at age nine. She soon joined Brazil's national indoor volleyball team. The talented setter helped Brazil finish seventh at the 1980 Olympics when she was 18 years old. She was a member of the 1984 Olympic team that also finished seventh.

Silva and Pires began playing together in the early 1990s. Silva was 11 years older than Pires, and she helped her less experienced partner. After the 1996 Olympics, Silva and Pires won the 1997 World Championship. The pair split in 1998.

Winning gold at the 1996 Olympics meant that Silva had won every major international beach volleyball tournament. She was one of the best beach volleyball players in the world when she retired in 2004. Pires won a bronze medal with Adriana Samuel at the 2000 Olympics in Sydney, Australia. She competed in the 2004 Olympics in Athens, Greece, with Ana Paula Connelly, but they did not win a medal.

Brazil has been one of the most enthusiastic supporters and successful nations for beach volleyball. At the Olympics in 1996, 2000, and 2004, Brazilian teams won five of the nine medals awarded. The two Brazilian teams

Big in Brazil

Shelda Bede and Adriana Behar of Brazil were the favorites heading into the 2000 Olympics. The team was considered the best in the world at the time. They had been atop the world rankings since 1997. But Australians Natalie Cook and Kerri Pottharst defeated them in the gold-medal match.

Afterward, the Brazilians apologized to their fans. Bede cried. Beach volleyball is taken very seriously in Brazil. Only soccer is more popular. Their somber mood reminded fans that beach volleyball was not just for fun. It was competitive, especially at the Olympics.

The Brazilians would get redemption. They defeated Cook and her new partner at the 2004 Olympics and also won a silver medal.

▲ *Holly McPeak competes in an AVP tournament in Huntington Beach, California.*

playing at the 2008 Olympics in Beijing, China, finished fourth and tied for fifth.

HOLLY MCPEAK

Holly McPeak was the first U.S. star of beach volleyball. McPeak grew up in Manhattan Beach in Southern California. She played in her first beach volleyball tournament in 1987 at age 19. McPeak was a star at the University of California, Los Angeles, playing indoor volleyball. She helped her team win a college national championship in 1990, her only year playing there. She became a full-time beach volleyball player in 1992.

The Californian won her first beach tournament in 1993. Her team was favored to win gold at the 1996 Olympics. However, an upset left them tied for fifth and without a medal.

McPeak remained one of the top players on the U.S. and world tours. Next, she teamed with Misty May-Treanor at the 2000 Olympics in Sydney and tied for fifth. McPeak competed in the Olympics in Athens four

Wearing Bikinis

Most female beach volleyball players wear bikinis to compete. This uniform has caused controversy, as some people believe that women's volleyball won't be taken seriously if the players look too sexy.

Holly McPeak weighed in on the issue in a *Sports Illustrated* interview in 1997. "If people want to come check us out because they're scoping our bodies, I don't have a problem with that, because I guarantee they'll go home talking about our athleticism."

Holly McPeak and other players of the late 1990s helped launch beach volleyball into the spotlight, making it the popular sport it is now.

years later. With her new partner Elaine Youngs, she lost to May-Treanor and Kerri Walsh in the semifinals. Then, McPeak and Youngs defeated Australians Natalie Cook and Nicole Sanderson in the bronze-medal game.

When McPeak retired in 2009, she had won a then-record 72 beach volleyball titles. She was the first woman volleyball player to earn more than $1.5 million in her career. "She's had an amazing career to say the very least, and helped pioneer the sport for us ladies," said Walsh. Playing together, Walsh and May-Treanor later broke McPeak's consecutive-win record.

BEACH SUCCESS

In 1997, FIVB held its first official beach volleyball World Championships. Within a year, 120 nations held organized beach volleyball activities.

The 2000 Olympics built on beach volleyball's success from its debut at the 1996 Olympics. The 2000 Olympics were in Sydney, Australia. The beach volleyball stadium was built on Bondi Beach, near Sydney. The laid-back atmosphere from Atlanta continued in Sydney. Fans who filled the 10,000-seat stadium heard rock music blare between points.

The men's and women's tournaments each had 24 teams. The Brazilian teams were expected to dominate the women's competition as they had done in Atlanta.

Instead, the Australian team of Kerri Pottharst and Natalie Cook upset Brazil's Adriana Behar and Shelda Bede in the gold-medal game.

Brazil took a 10–6 lead, but the Australians came back to win. In the next game, the Brazilians took another 10–6 lead. The Australians came back again, thanks to Pottharst's strong serve and Cook's consistency and energy. They won the second game to take home gold. Later, Pottharst and Cook were given Australia's highest honor, the Order of Australia.

Stars from Down Under

Natalie Cook and Kerri Pottharst were the stars of Australia for many years. They won a bronze medal at the first Olympic beach volleyball tournament in 1996.

The two star players split up after the 1996 Olympics. At the 2000 Olympics, however, the pair decided to face the favored Brazilian team together. This decision paid off with Olympic gold.

They both came back to the 2004 Olympics in Athens with different partners. Pottharst and partner Summer Lochowicz finished ninth. Cook and partner Nicole Sanderson finished fourth. Cook and a new partner, Tamsin Barnett, finished tied for fifth at the 2008 Olympics in Beijing, China. Pottharst did not compete.

Seeing Gold

To prepare for the 2000 Olympics, Australians Natalie Cook and Kerri Pottharst surrounded themselves with the color gold. They had fake gold medals, goldfish, gold toothpaste, and gold shampoo. Something they did worked. The Australian pair won the gold medal.

Beach volleyball underwent some changes in 2002. The outdoor sport switched to rally scoring. In rally scoring, either team can score during a rally, similar to indoor volleyball. Prior to the rule change, only the serving team could score. The size of the court was also decreased to 52.5 feet by 26.2 feet (16 m by 8 m).

▲ *Australians Kerri Pottharst (left) and Natalie Cook celebrate their gold-medal win at the 2000 Olympics.*

▲ *The U.S. indoor volleyball team won silver at the 2008 Olympics.*

CHAPTER 5

PLAYING TO WIN

U.S. success in volleyball has inspired new spectators and players across the country. The U.S. women's indoor team won a silver medal at the 2008 Olympics in Beijing, China. College indoor volleyball is quickly becoming one of the most popular sports across the nation. And Misty May-Treanor and Kerri Walsh have attracted many new fans to beach volleyball.

GOING FOR THE GOLD

The 2008 Olympics were emotional for the U.S. women's indoor volleyball team. Besides Coach Lang Ping's return to her homeland, the U.S. team also dealt with tragedy. During the first day of competition, the father of a former U.S. teammate was killed while visiting a tourist site in Beijing. Many of the women had played with Elisabeth "Wiz" Bachman McCutcheon on the 2004 Olympic team. The U.S. women players wrote "Wiz" on their arms and shoulders in support of their friend.

The U.S. team had only won two medals in the Olympics, taking a silver in 1984 and a bronze in 1992. The team

Collegiate Volleyball

Women's volleyball is becoming one of the most popular collegiate sports across the United States. Many schools attract thousands of fans to each game. The National Collegiate Athletic Association (NCAA) governs college sports. The NCAA held its first Women's Volleyball National Championship in 1981. The University of Southern California won that tournament. Teams from California and Hawaii won the first 14 NCAA championships. Teams from the Midwest and the South have improved since then and have had better showings. Some of the top programs in the country are at the University of Nebraska and Penn State.

had been top-ranked at the 2004 Olympics but failed to win a medal. In 2008, the U.S. women were ranked fourth in the world. This time, the players were determined to get one.

The U.S. team began the tournament by beating Japan. Next, however, it was swept by traditional power Cuba. The U.S. women came back with a win in their next match over Venezuela. Next was China, Lang's old team and the reigning Olympic champion. There was a thrilling five-set showdown in which all of the sets were close. The U.S. women were victorious. The team completed the preliminary round by beating Poland.

Any loss in the next rounds would end the U.S. team's hope for a medal. In the quarterfinals, they faced second-ranked Italy. The U.S. team fell behind 2–1 in sets. But Lindsey Berg's strong serving helped the U.S. team come back and win in five sets. Next, the U.S. players swept Cuba 3–0 in a rematch.

Last, they would face first-ranked Brazil in the gold-medal match. Brazil was a strong team and had not lost a single set in the tournament. The U.S. team won the third set against Brazil, but that was all. Brazil defeated the United States 3–1. Brazil had won its first Olympic gold medal in women's indoor volleyball. Although the U.S. players wanted to win the gold medal, they were gracious in defeat. "We definitely exceeded expectations

Logan Tom (bottom left) spikes the ball toward Brazilian blockers in the gold-medal game of the 2008 Olympics.

LOGAN TOM

Logan Tom was the star player for the U.S. indoor team at the 2008 Olympics. The 6 feet 1 inch (1.85 m) outside hitter scored 124 points and started all 33 sets her team played. She was named the tournament's best scorer.

Tom first gained national attention while in high school in Salt Lake City, Utah. She was a freshman at Stanford University in 1999 but took a break to compete in the 2000 Olympics. The 19 year old was the youngest member of the team. She returned to Stanford midway through her sophomore season in 2000. The Stanford team won the NCAA championship in 2001.

Tom came into the 2004 Olympics as the star U.S. player. She led the team to a fifth-place finish. Tom then left indoor volleyball. She quickly adapted to the beach game. Tom was named Rookie of the Year during her first year on the AVP tour. She rejoined the U.S. indoor team after three years. In 2008, Tom led the U.S. indoor team to second place. This was its best finish in the Olympics since 1984, when it also had finished second.

▲ *Logan Tom attacks the ball at the 2008 Olympics.*

of others, but deep down inside we knew we could be here," Berg said. "Definitely the tragedy . . . brought us even closer. Beating China brought us closer. We just kept growing from there and definitely improved as a team each match."

BEACH STARS

U.S. players have gotten stronger and better at each Olympics since beach volleyball was introduced. After a slow start at the first two Olympics, the United States produced two of the most successful players in the sport's history. Misty May-Treanor and Kerri Walsh dominated the sport from 2001 until 2009. They were elite athletes and popular celebrities.

Both women were born in California. Both starred as indoor volleyball players before turning to beach volleyball. May-Treanor was born in Los Angeles and attended Long Beach State. She helped her team go undefeated and win the NCAA championship in 1998. May-Treanor began focusing on beach volleyball after college. She teamed with Holly McPeak to finish fifth in the 2000 Olympics.

Walsh was born in Santa Clara. She played indoor volleyball at Stanford University. There, she led her team to an NCAA championship during her first two seasons, 1996 and 1997. She was considered one of the best college volleyball players of all time. Walsh joined the U.S.

indoor team after college. She was a right side hitter at the 2000 Olympics, where the team finished fourth.

May-Treanor and Walsh began competing together as a beach volleyball team in 2001. Walsh had never played competitive beach volleyball before, and May-Treanor had only played for one year. But, they quickly became the world's dominant beach volleyball team. They would remain the top-ranked team for the next seven years. The pair enjoyed record winning streaks while competing in AVP and FIVB tours. They were world champions in 2003, 2005, and 2007.

Most casual fans learned of the team at the 2004 Olympics. Beach volleyball was again extremely popular at those Olympics in Athens, Greece. May-Treanor and Walsh were the stars. May-Treanor did not play in the

Beach Volleyball in China

China has long been a powerhouse of indoor volleyball. But China showed at the 2008 Olympics that it has star beach volleyball players, too. China's two teams won the silver and bronze medals while competing in front of their home fans. The nation's best finish before 2008 was the round of 16, in 2000 and 2004. "I believe that today we have made a historical breakthrough in beach volleyball," said Wang Jie after she won the silver medal in 2008 with Tian Jia.

months before the Olympics because of an injury. Despite this, the team did not lose a set in all seven matches they played. May-Treanor and Walsh became the first U.S. women to win a gold medal in beach volleyball.

Fans loved watching May-Treanor and Walsh. The women were great athletes and had fun on the court. They stayed strong after the 2004 Olympics. The pair entered the 2008 Olympics ranked second. They were in the midst of a record winning streak. And they were determined to defend their gold medal.

The Californians cruised past their first-round opponents at the 2008 Olympics in Beijing, China. They fell behind in the first game against Belgians Liesbeth Mouha and Liesbet van Breedam, but managed to pull out a win.

Nicole Branagh (left) and Kerri Walsh compete in 2009.

NEW STAR

U.S. beach volleyball player Nicole Branagh began as a star indoor player. She competed for the U.S. indoor team from 2001 until 2003 before switching to beach volleyball in 2004. She was named Rookie of the Year in 2005. Branagh partnered with Elaine Youngs at the 2008 Olympics and tied for fifth. Branagh was the Most Valuable Player on the 2009 AVP tour. She has partnered with Kerri Walsh and also joined Misty May-Treanor on the AVP tour at the start of the 2010 season. At 6 feet 2 inches (1.88 m) tall, Branagh is strong at the net. The AVP named her the 2009 Offensive Player of the Year.

They won their semifinal match and moved on to the final round to play for the gold.

May-Treanor and Walsh met top-seeded Tian Jia and Wang Jie of China in the gold-medal match. Rain poured down on the players as they took to the sand. The stadium was filled with enthusiastic fans. But hometown fans would not see another gold medal for China. Preferring well-placed shots to powerful spikes, May-Treanor and Walsh defeated the Chinese pair 21–18 and 21–18.

May-Treanor and Walsh became the first team to win two gold medals in Olympic beach volleyball. Their 112-match winning streak was broken shortly after the 2008 Olympics. It had lasted for more than a year. The pair split in 2009. May-Treanor appeared on the popular television show *Dancing with the Stars*. Walsh took time off to give birth to her first child. The legends hope to reunite at some point "and be better than ever," Walsh said.

Women players indoors and out make volleyball an exciting sport to watch. But volleyball is even more fun when you play yourself. So grab a ball and get out there!

▲ Kerri Walsh (left) and Misty May-Treanor celebrate their beach volleyball gold medal at the 2008 Olympics.

GLOSSARY

attack: An offensive shot that sends the ball toward the other team's court.

block: A defensive move in which frontcourt players stop the ball with their raised arms. A block does not count as one of the team's three hits.

boycotted: Refused to participate as a form of protest.

debuted: Happened for the first time.

dig: A defensive move that stops the ball from hitting the ground in the defender's court.

dink: A soft shot that gets past the other team's blockers.

elite: At the top of one's sport or profession.

federations: Groups of smaller organizations that come together to be run by one central government or committee.

intensely: With great strength or difficulty.

missionaries: People sent to another country to spread religious beliefs and do social work.

pass: A contact with the ball that sends the ball to a teammate.

professional: Playing at an advanced level for money.

rally: The time the ball is in play, between the serve and when the ball hits the ground or a team has an error.

serve: The first contact in a rally that puts the ball into play.

set: A contact that positions the ball for an attack shot; also a term for a single volleyball game.

spike: A type of attacking shot in which the player hits the ball hard toward the floor in the opponent's court.

sponsors: People or companies that provide money or services to support a league or player.

versatile: Able to do many things well.

FOR MORE
INFORMATION

BOOKS

Beeson, Chris. *Volleyball*. Broomall, PA: Mason Crest, 2004.
This book covers volleyball history and rules, as well as training, common injuries, and how to become a professional player.

Crisfield, Deborah. *Winning Volleyball for Girls*. New York: Facts on File, 2002.
This book includes detailed diagrams of volleyball rules and techniques.

Dann, Sarah. *Volleyball in Action*. New York: Crabtree, 2000.
This book explains volleyball rules, techniques, and equipment.

Miller, Bob. *The Volleyball Handbook*. Champaign, IL: Human Kinetics, 2005.
Written by a high school coach, this book teaches the finer details of the sport.

USA Volleyball. *Volleyball Systems & Strategies*. Champaign, IL: Human Kinetics, 2009.
This training guide features dozens of drills to put players at the top of their game.

WEB SITES

Association of Volleyball Professionals
www.avp.com
This Web site features information that includes statistics, player biographies, and calendars of AVP events.

FIVB
www.fivb.org
The official Web site of the International Volleyball Federation includes volleyball history, player information, and international volleyball news.

USA Volleyball
www.volleyball.teamusa.org
The official Web site of the U.S. Olympic team features news, blog posts, and other information.

INDEX

PLACES TO VISIT

The Olympic Museum

1, quai d'Ouchy
1006 Lausanne
Switzerland
+41 21 621 6511
www.olympic.org/en/content/The-Olympic-Museum/
The Olympic Museum in Switzerland features exhibits on all
aspects of Olympics history. The Web site includes virtual tours
and exhibits.

The Volleyball Hall of Fame

444 Dwight St, Holyoke, MA 01040
413-536-0926
www.volleyhall.org
The Volleyball Hall of Fame features exhibits and interactive
videos. It also hosts tournaments and other volleyball-related
events.

ABOUT THE AUTHOR

 Chrös McDougall is a sportswriter and author.
He covered the University of Missouri women's
volleyball team for two seasons while working
for a local newspaper, and also covered Olympic
sports for various organizations. He lives in
Minnesota with his wife.

ABOUT THE CONTENT CONSULTANT

 Mike Hebert is the head coach of the University
of Minnesota women's volleyball team. Under
Hebert, the team made its first appearance in the
national championship game in 2004. Hebert
coached Lindsey Berg, who was on the U.S.
Olympic indoor team in 2004, and Nicole Branagh,
who played beach volleyball in the 2008 Olympics.